WINGLESS ANGEL

Wingless Angel

Written by **Ralph Watkins**

First American
Book In Print

Poetry and Prose
Keeping it Real

Publisher: AUDAX, LLC.
Reserved copyright 2014
Email: dmvpoet@gmail.com
Published District Heights, M.D
Print In America September 2019

Preface

First edition of a book written by Ralph Watkins Jr.
designed for family, friends, and people of mature
age; that love reading modern, and urban literary cre-
ative work. Which embodies thoughts, feelings, and
emotions. Often reflecting on life, family, and rela-
tionships experiences; copyright 1994 and 2014 RAW
Material in a text.

The body of work stretches over 40 years, from ear-
ly childhood to present, which encompasses and de-
picts various life situations. Poetry has always been a
useful tool to share, and encourage others. And it also
builds bridges between two different places, to give
people an easier and safer passage through words on
a page.

 One of my biggest dreams goes as far back as I can
remember, and that is to be a creative writer of po-
etry and short stories. I did not take a direct path,
and I was not always focused. But my heart was al-
ways in the right place. In my heart, I kept this love
for writing poetry alive.

Over the years I would revisit the thought of writing
a complete book of poetry. I have arrived at a place in
my heart, whereas I no longer want to put off my
dream until tomorrow. Good luck my friends in your
travels through this world.

Table of Contents

GOD'S KINGDOM

God's Kingdom
is too good
for me.

But, it won't
stop me from
trying to
better myself.

I know I don't
want to go to hell.
I want to live my
life in eternity.

Lord, make me clean.
Help me to see, and to know
that you always have better for
me.

I WOULD NOT

I would not have you ignorant, the hour is drawing near when it will be-come too late to save yourselves or better yet, the ones you love.

Many of us don't love ourselves enough to stop doing the things which we know are wrong, seek salvation; or stay woke long enough in church to get saved.

So, we along with our children will come running and screaming at hours end, pounding on the church doors but the churches as we knew them, will be no more; with corrupted Teachers, Preachers and Prophets falsifying God's word.

MY FIRST MISTAKE

My first mistake, I went high, when I should have gone low. When I had them in my grasp, I shouldn't have let them go.

I couldn't sleep last night. I was out there running. I had gotten lost someplace in S.E., D.C., that I've never been before. I was climbing and jumping fences.

I didn't think that I was running from anything or anyone at first, but all that changed after my conscience started catching up with me. I saw people I knew from years ago. I asked them, I had to ask them, to cover me.

I'm thinking about all the things I've done, I shouldn't have done, when I knew in my good conscience I was wrong.

I ran into a haven of people inside of a marching parade, surrounded by old people rallying at the end for their cause, holding each other up, literally carrying their own bed. All when I thought it was safe to do so again, I took off running.

I purposely avoided juvenile delinquents' in the street along my path, figuring they'd leave me alone because of my displacement and gray hair, I assumed right. I was allowed again to take refuge in countless homes throughout the night, of many who did not know me, just estimated my plight. I woke up wondering, what was this all about? I'll let you know later.

JUST THINK

Just think, if you had your chance but you chose differently. You didn't once consider yourself or love your children enough to take them by the hand and lead them in God's direction.

Just imagine, by you helping others you would have been saved as well.

God's love is wrapped up in His promise, that if you accept me as your Lord and Savior and live according to my word, I will give you life more abundantly, and also share eternity with you.

IT'S NOT MY INTENT

It's not my intent to insult your intelli-
gence, but it was and wasn't me at the
same time. It's not that I have no recol-
lection of the truth, but a slight error
has occurred.

I would not and could not do or bring
harm without a temporary leave of my
conscious mind or senses.

Yes, it is me who pleads but also who is
totally unaware at the time of the inci-
dent, for which I plead, "Not guilty."
Every man cannot be at fault or to blame
when he or she makes a fatal mistake.

All I remember was hearing them say, "I
don't love you anymore." And I was con-
sciously awakened when the gun fell
from my alleged hands hit the floor.

THE SHOES OF A MAN

The shoes of a man are both his heart and soul.
They know the story of his life, everywhere he's
been and how he continues moving forward.
When you've been in such a relationship, it's
hard to start over with anyone else or anything
else. Even if they don't look or feel like a good
fit.
From the time you wake up in the morning and by
the end of your day, we often struggle for kind
words to say to each other, and sometimes this is
okay.
Everything in our lives wasn't made to last forev-
er. Don't take my word for it, just look around
you and in your past at the things and people that
are no longer there.
Things and people in our lives suffer so much
wear and tare. You can't always so easily discard
them like socks and underwear.
So, it's not with jealousy or envy but in admira-
tion that you're able to manage a pair of shoes
this long.
My ignorance, but while I was going through life,
I had forgotten the real meaning of being in a
meaningful relationship. Just makes me realize, I
have even further to go and things to learn in
these unbroken-in pair of shoes.

WHAT IF

What if
you woke up tomorrow,
and couldn't talk?
And later that same day
you couldn't walk.
What if in
that same day
you wanted to,
but could not cry?
What if
all along
you knew
that God was
always trying
to tell you something,
but you ignore all
His warning signs,
you kept
right on going.
You know green light
means go, but
you're proceeding
without caution
through the red light.
In your REARVIEW mirror
it's blurring.
What if tomorrow you wake up
too late for you to listen
TO ALL GOD'S WARNINGS.

SOME OF US

For some of us the clouds never did open up, and the sun never did shine. They only saw and felt the rain, and cried and complained.
Because it never seemed to have stopped, even during God's most graceful moments;e they kept their heads covered, and continued to cry and com-plained, about how awful God is and the weather we are having.

These same people have a way of making our lives dreary, and I am thankful for every day and all that God gives me.

TOMORROW

I THANK YOU FOR YOUR KIND WORDS
AND FLOWERS. I WISH I COULD EX-
PRESS ALL THE FEELINGS I HAVE AND
THE HEARTFELT SENTIMENT.

FOR SOME IT WAS ON THE PLAY-
GROUND, NEIGHBORHOOD FRIENDS
AND OTHERS IT WAS A CASUAL BY
CHANCE AQUAINTANCES.

I JUST WISH WE COULD HAVE SPENT
A LITTLE MORE TIME TOGETHER.
WHERE DID ALL THE TIME GO? COUNT-
LESS PROMISES THAT WE WOULD
HOOK-UP, PLAY CATCH-UP, OR HANG
OUT.

FUNNY, HOW I CAN LAUGH ABOUT IT
NOW? BECAUSE I KNOW IT DOESNT
HAVE TO END THIS WAY, WITH ME
LAYING DOWN OR WITH YOU LOOK-
ING UP AT ME.

THIS IS A DAY TOO LATE

And this stage is not big enough and I am not one that feels worthy enough to speak about a man whose shoes no can fill. From birth to death, he came into the world fighting for his survival, fought for the things he was taught to believe in, on the city street where he grew up, and he took that same courageous fight onto the battlefield on foreign soil; when he served in the U.S. Army. My dad Ralph A. Watkins Sr. was a Man of Valor.

He stood-up and believe in peaceful resolutions, with very few words and no second chances, it's now or never. He defended himself, fought for others, and he would leap off into any direction beyond his reach to protect anyone in trouble. Those that knew him, would say he was a column holding up a community.

I have seen him in many lights, some brighter than 10,000 angels gathering, when he spoke or wrote about the goodness of God, and then there were the moments that was not so bright for him. But he always managed to smile and encourage everyone around him to do the right things so God will show favor upon you one day.

My dad was and always will be a Bridge Builder, a person that made a way for others to cross over troubled waters in the world, and the life afterward.

A MOMENT

A moment to reflect.
Had I been there,
in my child's life?
Or am I constantly
trying to play catch-up,
leaving a trail of breadcrumb
of broken promises, and
years of unnecessary neglect.

It's never too late while you
still have a breath of air
but the child or children
may no longer care, because
them and mommy have
managed quite well
without you being there.

So, Happy Father's Day to
the absentee dad, for
being the father I never had.
I will be better than you.
I will be there for my child,
day and night, and help them
with whatever they have to go through
in life.

LIFE CAN BE FUNNY

Life can be funny, life can be sad, and it can also be strange. Two people meet as strangers and spend a lot of time trying to get to know each other.

Some people spend years doing this and end up like they started out, strangers. They really don't know each other like they thought. Take as much time as you need to truly get to know a person.

Don't rush into anything, just because people say life is too short. Some scars last a lifetime and for most people that's too long.

LOVE LEADS TO INSANITY

Be careful who you love and who loves you. Sometimes we lose ourselves in the process of building relationships.

And the ones that love us make us become someone that we are not, either their slave or someone they worship.

Being in love can make you crazy because you want the companionship, but the big picture or somewhere down the road, someone is going to end up dead or in a mental institution.

So be careful, there are a lot of nuts out there, and you don't need one to make you one their substitution.

TO MY CHILDREN

I've always wondered what to tell my children when they ask. Who am I? What am I doing here? I believe to have been led by the spirit when to inform them. That we are all here on a mission. You must love God and follow His commandments, and try to live a sinless and an upright life.

In our lives, most people are attracted to different religious persuasions, but I submit that it's not important what church that you attend a church or none at all, but pursue the knowledge of why you are in this world.

And live your life to fulfill that obligation, you will reap the benefits of your commitment just as everyone else; you were recorded upon entrance into the world as Sons of God in training.

I do not have anything against attending regular church services. It affords me the opportunity to not only lay aside the cares of preceding days but also to be coached in the proper morality one must assume, that help us in making the right choices that affect our lives. In addition, I just as our offspring are born with our physical attributes and the animal-like bodies that clothes us.

THERE'S NOTHING

THERE'S NOTHING OUT HERE
FOR THOSE LOOKING FOR
LOVE AND SEX.
BOTH ARE OVERRATED
LIKE A CANDLE IN THE DARK.

IT BURNS BRIGHT BUT
WHEN DAY BREAKS
YOU DON'T NEED IT ANYMORE.

YOU STILL HAVE TO EAT,
YOU STILL HAVE TO WORK
IN ORDER TO MAINTAIN.

IF YOU'RE GOING TO KEEP
A ROOF OVER YOUR HEAD,
GO BACK TO THE BASIC. FIND GOD
BEFORE IT'S TOO LATE.

HIS DOOR, ARM, AND HEART
ARE ALWAYS OPEN. CHURCH IS A
GOOD PLACE TO START BUT
YOU HAVE TO SUBMIT
AND OPEN YOUR HEART BEFORE YOU DEPART.

MY WINGLESS ANGEL

I have tried all my life to earn a set of wings for my deserving angel. As I look at you, it brought tears to my eyes. I wasn't trying to keep you earthbound, this is me being the best person I can be, I know I have to do better.

I don't want my angel walking around aimlessly each day like me. Wondering how I am going to make it through another Winter with this bitter weather. I am saving my change so we can take a Winter vacation, rethink some things and have a better relationship.

I can see me joining a church and possibly their choir, once inside I will sing. This might help bring people closer to Christ, save a soul or two, and you'll earn both your wings, then you can go help save someone, other than me.

CREATION OF MAN

We all have a spiritual body that inhabits the one that we see. Now follow me, this spiritual body has a similar role. It was designed to transport our souls.

There is a popular belief that circulates around the story that man was banished from the Garden of Eden after eating fruit from a tree. I submit, unless heaven as we know, it is a physical world, there would be no Garden, no tree, and consequences no fruit.

To believe that is to believe that God would make a mistake when he created man in his image, created with all of Gods powers.

Since, when reading the reports of the creation of man, God did not say, "It is good!" He did with the rest of creation; the creation of man was incomplete. Perceiving this as a possibility, that we were given the opportunity to assist in our own perfection.

I TRIED TO DO EVERYTHING

I tried within my Superman powers to be there for you. I woke up one day and you were gone. I still couldn't figure out what I did wrong, so I called my best friends, Lil Wayne, Akron, Wale and Drake to help put some words together and sing you this, I need you back in my world song. I need you to forget about all my past mistakes, I want to dance more than Drake.

I served my time and I learned from my past mistakes, the difference between right and wrong, but I never stop writing I love you in a song and signing each one Akon.

I know you don't think I have learned from past mistakes and don't feel my pain, but without you, I have been going crazy like Lil Wayne. Please call me baby, so we can start all over again.

BEFORE SCHOOL

I am trying to get my teenage son out
the door for school. While I am stand-
ing here and pressing his clothes, from
out of nowhere, I can smell weed.

My head popped up like a deer in the
headlights. I am thinking someone has
started the party without me. I looked
around and none of my doors or windows
are opened.

It has my nostrils wide open, wondering
where the heck this smell is coming
from? I continued to press out my son's
clothes, and then I am hit with the
steam bouncing from his clothes.

After further investigation, the shirt
was made in Columbia. He'll be wearing
another shirt this morning for school.

TOO COOL

Too cool,
to be a fool,
had to stay
in school,
respect my
peers and teachers
and follow all
the rules.
There will always be
time to make or break
crazy shots on the
basketball court or
in a game of pool,
because if we don't take advantage
of an education, life is going
to have you pushing a shopping
cart with all your worldly belonging.
Education is the key that will open
many doors, but you can't always just
show up, you have to know your tools.

I AM GOING TO TELL IT

I feel like God has
this hedge around me,
it does not allow me
to go too far, and
it protects me from
intruders.
No one can see it, not
even me, but I know
it's there.
My angels are
within the camp,
and they keep me
from falling,
when I feel
angst for any reason.
God knows when it's me
that's calling.
Lord, I see
and hear people
their pain,
lift them up,
and heal their
body, mind, and spirit,
IN JESUS NAMES

IT HURTS NOW

IT HURTS NOW
BUT THE PAIN
DOES GOES AWAY.
IT TAKES TIME
TO HEAL.

I KNOW PEOPLE LOOK
AT ME AND THEY
WILL SEE A RIVER OF TEARS.

BUT I KNOW ONCE
I GET MYSELF TOGETHER
I WILL BE BACK ON TOP
OF THE HILL.

BEING IN THE GAME, ON
FIRST AND SECOND DOWN,
IS THE LIFE I LIVE.

EVEN AFTER I GET BANDAGED UP,
I AM GOING BACK ONTO
THE FIELD.

IN THE SAME HOUSE

WE LIVE IN THE SAME HOUSE
BUT WHEN I GET UP OUT OF BED
WE SNUB EACH OTHER LIKE WE
LIVE IN A GATED COMMUNITY.

YOU ACT LIKE YOUR CHILDREN
ARE BETTER THEN MY CHILDREN.
HAVE YOU FORGOTTEN, IT'S A
BLENDED FAMILY AND WE SAID,
WE'D NEVER LET THEM FEEL THE
DIFFERENCE.

I THINK WE NEED TO FIND A
WAY TO MAKE THIS THING
WORK, STOP THINKING SINGLE
MINDED, OR WE WILL BOTH
MISS OUR BLESSING AND END UP
BLINDED.

I KNOW CRAZY PEOPLE

I live with one, I work with some and a lot of them are my closet friends I often stop and look in the mirror for a long period of time before I leave out in the morning and ask myself, "Are you ok?" When I really think about it, it was like a slow opening door and as I got closer, I got snatched in.

So, I take meds three times a day, and some days I forget to take them and other days I feel like I can go without them. I start off talking to myself when no one else is in the room, and when someone else walks in the room, I don't want them to them I was talking about them, so I just don't stop talking.

I have had my moments when no one seems to be listening to me or understands a word I saying. But it does not require three to four people trying to restrain me, and telling me it's going to be okay, "We are going to take you to a place where people can try to help you."

I didn't want to be helped; I was fine living in the world I was in. Now, I am sitting up here, supposedly with my head on straight and my life intact, at work dealing with nothing but crazy people.

CHEERING SECTION

EVERYONE ONE OF US HAS THEIR OWN
CHEERING SECTION. SOME OF US HAVE
AS MANY AS A CROWD OF 50,000 AS
YOU TAKE TO THE FIELD, FRIENDS,
FAMILY, AND ADMIRED FANS.

 BUT MINES HAS ALWAYS BEEN MY
GRANDMOTHER, SITTING AT HOME, IN
A SETTLED IN LITTLE CHAIR. SEWING
OR READING HER BIBLE, AND I KNOW
WHERE EVER I AM IN THE WORLD, MY
GRANDMA' IS PRAYING OR ROOTING
FOR ME, "GO BABY! GO!"

I CAN NOT ASK FOR A BIGGER CHEER-
ING SECTION THAN HER, BECAUSE SHE
ALWAYS HAS MY BACK, EVEN AFTER THE
LIGHTS GO OFF, AND EVERY ONE ELSE
HAS GONE HOME. THAT'S WHY I LOVE
MY GRANDMOTHER SO VERY MUCH!"

WINGLESS ANGEL

HE SEEMED ANGRY

ON GOOD AND BAD DAYS, IT DIDNT SEEM TO MATTER IF
THE SUN WAS UP OR THE MOON WAS GLOWING. IF AND
WHEN HE WAS IN A BAD MOOD NOTHING DIDNT MAT-
TER.

I WAS THINKING BECAUSE HIS DAD DIED WHEN HE
WAS OF A VERY YOUNG AGE, I CAN SEE WHERE THAT
COULD CAUSE A LITTLE HOSTILITY AND SOME INNER
RAGE, I KNOW HE VOLUNTEERED TO FIGHT IN A WAR HE
DIDNT START OR UNDERSTAND AT A VERY YOUNG AGE.

I SAW A LOT OF THINGS THAT HE KEPT INSIDE, AND
WHENEVER HE TOLD STORIES OF WAR, THERE WERE
MANY TIMES HE'D JUST SKIP THE PAGE. I LOVED HIM
MANY TIMES WHEN I WAS ANGRY WITH HIM AND I
DIDNT UNDERSTAND, HOW A MAN THAT COULD BE CON-
SIDERED A GENTLE GIANT, ALWAYS DID HIS BEST WORK
ON STAGE.

BUT BEHIND THE SCENE, HE'D YELL, AND SCREAM. I NEED
A DRINK. A PACK CIGARETTE AND FOR EVERYONE THAT'S
STANDING AROUND TO TAKE THIS COSTUME OFF OF ME.

EVEN AT HIS WORST, HE WAS BETTER THAN MOST, BE-
CAUSE HE NEVER ABANDONED SHIP AND NO MATTER
WHAT, IN FACE OF MANY OF LIFE'S ADVERSITIES, HE
ALWAYS STOOD TALL AND SAID, THE SHOW MUST GO
ON. AND FOR THOSE THAT DIDNT KNOW OR UNDER-
STAND MY DAD, AT THOSE CERTAIN MOMENTS, I HOPE
YOU LIKE HE DID, JUST TURN THE PAGE.

I HAVE ASKED MYSELF

I HAVE ASKED MYSELF, AM I SUPPOSED TO BE HERE? THE SON THAT ALWAYS THROUGH TEMPER TANTRUMS WHEN THINGS DIDN'T GO THEIR WAY.

THE BROTHER THAT COULDN'T KEEP UP WALKING TO THE CORNER STORE, CHURCH OR TO GRANDMA'S HOUSE, AND FAILDED FURTHER BEHIND IN MY REMEDIAL MATH AND READING.

NO MATTER HOW MUCH I TRIED, I ALWAYS WANTED TO BE THE SON A FATHER WOULD LOVE, AND SMILE EVERY TIME I MAKE EVERY EFFORT TO SEE ME TRY. FOR ALL THE TIMES THAT WERE IMPORTANT, MY DAD WAS THERE TO ENCOURAGE ME.

THIS IS ABOUT ME NOT GIVING UP, HANGING IN THERE WHEN I DON'T FEEL LIKE I AM MAKING A DIFFERENCE, BECAUSE I AM WHO I AM, AND I DO THE THINGS I DO BECAUSE MY MOM AND DAD MADE ALL THE DIFFERENCE IN THE WORLD. AND IT WAS MORE TO IT THAN JUST BEING THERE.

MY HITTER, MY HITTER

I always run like I just stole Third base -
My hitter, my hitter I am not stopping on
Third base, when I can hear my moms call-
ing me to run home. Blood dripping and
ravaged torn clothes, the lights and sirens
are following me like I did something
wrong.

I was running like I always do, but when
they started pointing at me. What else was
I suppose to do? I prayed and eulogized
myself all in one breath. "Lord forgives me
for all the things I've ever done wrong," as
I was struck in my side. I heard someone
say, "Stop running!" If they knew me, it
feels like I'm having a bad dream and I
can't wake up.

As I was lying there as close to death as
one can get, I'm thinking, this is one of the
best runs I've ever had. Note to self,
there's no way I can outrun the stupidity
of some cops with a gun.

CHANCES

I don't have a lot of chances that I can give to someone that's not trying to improve their lives or my life.

I don't have a lot of chances to give to anyone that keeps lying and wouldn't tell the truth if it were smacking them in the face.

I don't have any more chances to give to any-one that's always crying about how life is al-ways beating them down, and they just want to lean on me for just a little while.

Well, I think their best chances of winning with me, would be better spent on a lottery pick be-cause I'm all out of chances that I can give.

I NEED TO GO FOR A RIDE

I need to go for a ride. I kind of have an idea which direction I want to go. This is not about not knowing which way to turn. It's been a long time since I was there, back in time.

I know you won't be there, but the memories of what was, will be, still standing like tall buildings worn over time.
You were my yesterday, and a part of me that I can never forget, but always a part of me that I will always regret.

I know when I go back, you won't be there, but the memories of you will never escape. I hope I don't keep the memories of you waiting too long. I need to go for a ride.

MY PASTOR

As my Pastor would say, "Some of yall are not going to get this." While you're not doing what you're supposed to be doing, things are happening around us, whereas you should be in church or in prayer all the time.

I realize today that someone can hit a home run inside the park, and it has the same results as someone smacking that ball out of the Ball Park.

Either way, it really hurts. When God says, it's time to come home, it doesn't matter how you hit the ball. It's just that some of us never expect it when it does happen. "Amen ceiling."

PLEASE DON'T

Please don't make me a stranger, or someone you'd love to hate. Don't base all your thoughts and feelings on what others may say of me or judge me on my past mistakes.

If your only and final thoughts are to lock me away from your life and mind; throw away the key.

Just keep this one round in your judgment chamber; imagine if the gun was pointed at your heart from someone you once loved and cared about.

It's hard to walk away from someone you love, it's even harder when you stay and they don't love you back.

I don't have any advice to offer in one of life's desperate cries for help, but to pray often that God releases you or touches their heart, whichever comes first.

WE ALL HAVE MADE BAD CHOICES

Some, we have to live with-
Some, we have to deal with-
Still the result of choices
we've undoubtedly made-
Some, you can't hide from.
Some, you can't run from or
cover-up with makeup or wear
with a smile.

Every choice you make today
is going to make a damning or
good difference tomorrow, so
be very playful who you eat, sleep
with or align yourselves up with.

In all of our lives, there's been at least one
person that has tried to teach or preach the
importance of making the right choices, and
how some of them can be unhealthy, detri-
mental and often very costly. The excuse is,
"I never saw it coming." Or, "They changed."
The after effect, live with it, deal with it
and try to make better choices the next
time.

ONE OF MANY MEN

Here I am, one of many men; someone's son, brother, father or husband. Standing in a lineup to appear before potential witnesses, then members of my peers; and a hard-hearted judge that doesn't even know me or give a shyt about who I am.

Here we go again, and it doesn't have to be this way; where almost everyone is looking for a conviction. We could have gone straight for once and avoided this avoidable outcome. I don't know who else to blame, other than myself?

With my hands locked behind my back. I am looking down and not forward to where I'm headed toward. So farewell to one world and hello to an altogether different life. Looking down because I know the God above is ashamed of me. Told me before, "I can open the door but only you can set yourself free." That I am the key." I am facing time I can't get back.

I am not looking forward, but I only have myself to blame. Even my conscience tried to warn me, and I ignored it. Maybe next time I'll listen. Don't let your lifestyle get you locked up and incarcerated, the wants and needs are not worth it. Life is too damn short to be confined behind within high fences, trimmed with barbed wire, iron bars and nothing to look at but other damn men.

POURING COLD WET RAIN

This time last year I could outpace myself, it reminded me of an earlier time in my life. I couldn't get away from the relationship that I had been in fast enough.

I kept my head up, and I swung my arms across my body and kept it moving, so no one could see the tears falling from my eyes, and the heavy heart that I was carrying. I just wanted to run so fast, until I was able to just disappear.

I don't see them anymore and they can't see me. I made it out of my valley, and it's nothing like a mountaintop view. The taste of rain is sweet, and I celebrate it with a victory.

ONE DAY

ONE DREAM
ONE MAN
SAID I'LL
OUTLIVE THROUGH
MY SEED
ONE DAY
ONE DREAM
THEY'LL SEE ME
STANDING STRONGER
THROUGH MY SON'S EYES
IT TOOK
MORE THAN
ONE DAY
ONE DREAM
ONE MAN
BUT STILL ONE SEED
FROM
ONE MAN
ONE DREAM
THAT HAD
PLANNED
TO BE HERE TODAY
NO MATTER
WHAT IT TOOK
MY SON
KEEPING THE FAITH
KEEP RUNNING
SO THE DREAM
OF ONE MAN
NEVER DIES_

I HEAR CRYING

I hear crying at night, we all cry, just at different times, and for certain reasons. And it's okay to cry, especially when you're feeling some kind of hurt inside, or outside your body, it's physical pain.

As you can best believe there's going to be someone that's going to ask, or investigates, why are you crying? Who has upset the apple cart of one God's children? Most people immediately say to you, before they know the reason why, in a spiritual sense, "That everything is going to be okay."

I love my mother and grandmother a million times over because they'd always go a lot further by telling you, "To get up! Go in the bathroom and wipe your face, and then come back, and let me tell you how we're going to fix this. Because your crying is not going to fix the problem."

As I've gotten older, I've heard my mother and grandmother crying, especially when they're in physical pain or they are feeling some kind of way on the inside. Of course, I would I ask, "Why are you crying, grandma?" And she would say, "Baby when you've lived as long as I have and been through as much as I have, you have to cry, but most of yall have nothing to cry about. Only God can fix this."

THE IT FACTOR

For every man that is accounted for, a day comes when he must die. It is a bittersweet thing to come into this world as a passenger never knowing how long your stay.

Everyone always says make yourself comfortable, go to school, get married, have some children and live a little.

All in the same breath, they fail to mention the time you will have to do all these things, to say you have experienced life and lived.

Because none of us knows the end or expiration date of our lives before we open up a can or two, and only have a taste of it, while others ride, slide, walk leisurely, run or stumble their way not knowing their final destination call.

I can't tell you anything any differently, just don't waste it, squander it, lose it and always be mindful of it. This is the only thing you will be freely given immeasurably until it ends. Find ways to live peacefully and thank the Lord for this one-way ticket through life.

LOOK OUT MAN

I was the lookout man for a man that's
doing time upstate 12/15, three square
meals a day and a soul mate.

When the cops came they surrounded
the place on every side. I didn't hear any
sirens, just wedding bells, and I wasn't
about to become another man's bride.

So, I am no longer the lookout man. I got
down on my knees and ask God, what's
His plan for my life? And I made my way
out of there.

I am sure my partner in crime is not too
happy about my inconvenient desire to
have a divine intervention. But, he could
have turned to God at any time such as I
did, "I need you, Lord, right now to save
me." And he did, I walked away and never
looked back.

GENERIC PRESCRIPTION

Generic Prescription but it'll work like the name brand. After taking two tablets you'll realize the man in your life is worse than a five-year-old child. He doesn't listen, very forgetful and he doesn't know how to accept no for an answer when mommy says, "I have a headache right now."

Men are still stuck on sight words, and you can't go out of order, because no matter what you flash in front of them, they'll keep saying, "Water." I couldn't be a woman, it's a job and I'd quit, just too big of a pool and I wouldn't want to pull from it.

Don't waste your time learning the man, just figure out how you feel and attitude with the man in your life. And if he's the primary cause of your headache, you have two options, to pack his stuff or pack your stuff and leave him until he grows up.

I FIGURED

I figure, if I stay home, lock the doors and turn off all the lights, I wouldn't get into any trouble. I will just sit here and write, and listen to the sounds outside. Not even two hours into my therapeutic day off I can hear yelling outside my window, and knocking on my door, "I know you're in there!"

I knew I forgot one other thing. I should have parked my vehicle several blocks away. I only went outside to let them know that this is a quiet zone community. Nonetheless, I started celebrating because they wanted me to help them finish a dime bag of weed, where it's now legal to roll and smoke in Colorado.

The Police pulled up minutes later to inform us that they had received a Disturbance Call from this resident. That was me. And the Officer reminded us after several citations, that this is not Colorado. And when they do legalize it, he'll come back and join us.

YOU WENT

You went from hot to cold, young to old, soft to stone. You said, you weren't in the mood, to leave you alone.

I don't get it, I gave it some thought, and tried to forget it. I don't want to do or say something and have to later regret it.

I am not nice and cool even after I come out of the pool. I am always on fire, always looking to satisfy my every desire.

I don't need soft spoken words, a gentle touch, or anyone jumping on top of me, you'd be doing way too much.

I need to know what's on your mind? I don't want to pursue happiness that's walking away from me. I would rather unhand cuff them from my brass bed, kiss them on the forehead and bid them farewell, or tell to go home.

If they don't want play with me, that'll be fine, because there's a hell of a lot more other fish in the sea.

WHERE ARE MY ANGELS?

Where are my angels now? I feel a storm coming my way, and it's too late for me to run or take refuge. I tried telling you that I love you. I tried drawing a picture of you and me in a house sitting on the front porch, living happily ever after. I remember getting on my knees and praying, until I couldn't weep anymore. I said to my lord, "She was handmade for me."

Whatever you ask Lord, that I will do." I don't know why it didn't work to my favor. If I were a betting man, I would not have betted against me. Well, she's gone, and the show is over. Found someone to help pack her bag and big enough to keep me from pulling on her to stay by the arm.

I am not about to get myself worked over by someone that doesn't feel the same way as I do towards them. I would have given her the sun, moon, and the stars; I just don't have it to give right now.

I ask God for favor, I wonder if this is the favor He thinks I was seeking? Maybe God saw something that I was too blind to see, and He's making space for someone special in my life. Thank you, Jesus!

WINGLESS ANGEL

WHEN I GET OUT

When I get out of this Prison that I am in, I am never running with the same crew, or staying in this same rat hole infested-place or doing the same things that got me in this place again.

I want to start off with a new objective, see things from a different perspective, and I want to hold it down with a real job, even if it doesn't seem very effective.

I still want the same type of woman that I can stick with me, doesn't care what I driven, admires but I will do whatever it takes to keep a roof over her head and food the plate; knows in her heart, that she is my ride and die chick, I come home to moma, because she is my queen.

It took a while for me to wake up to this realization. You have to pay your dues before folks leave you the "f" alone, and then you pray for your breakthrough from God so that you can get released back into civilization.

I always promise to do better, the next time I hope to. And, I am not just sitting here blowing smoke up your skirt, or trying to convince myself. I know I still have time to think this whole thing through. Nothing but time.

SOMETIMES

SOMETIMES WE HAVE TO LEAVE PEOPLE RIGHT
WHERE WE FOUND THEM, WITHOUT PURPOSE
AND SELF DIRECTION. AND WE KNOW OUR
LIVES ARE FAR BETTER OFF WITHOUT THEM,
SO WE THINK.

- ALL I EVER WANTED TO DO WAS TO MAKE
SOMEONE ELSE HAPPY, BRING THEM FLOWERS,
JUST SEE THEM SMILE. I DIDN'T NEED OR
WANT ANYTHING FOR MY TROUBLES, IT GAVE
ME JOY TO BRING INTO SOMEONE ELSES LIFE.

I DIDN'T TAKE THE TIME TO GET TO KNOW
THEM, THEY MADE ME FEEL MY WORTH WAS
FAR MORE THAN THEIRS, THEY WERE ALWAYS
THERE FOR ME, AND WHEN THE SHOE WAS ON
THE OTHER FOOT, I JUST FIGURED WITHOUT
A VISIT OR A PHONE CALL THAT THEY WOULD
BE OKAY.

-THIS IS WHO I AM, I DON'T WANT BE SOME-
ONE ELSE OR FOR CIRCUMSTANCES TO CHANGE
ME. I KNOW PEOPLE DON'T ALWAYS SEE THE
BIG PICTURE, AND WHEN THEY FEEL THEY'RE
DONE WITH ME, I OFTEN SEE THEM MONTHS
OR YEARS LATER, TELLING ME HOW MUCH THEY
MISS ME SINCE THEY'VE BEEN GONE.

CLOSE YOUR EYES

CLOSE YOUR EYES AND TELL ME WHAT YOU SEE.
-I SEE NOTHING BUT DARKNESS, STARING BACK
AT ME.
-IT HAS NO HANDS, ARMS OR LEGS
- JUST COMPLETE DARKNESS.
TELL ME WHAT YOU HEAR.
- I GREW UP IN A WORLD OF NOISE,
-SO THIS KIND OF SILENT IS DEAFENING
TO ME, I BECAME SCARED OF THE DARKNESS
AND FEARFUL OF WHAT I COULD HEAR OR SEE.
WHERE ARE YOU?
- I AM ASLEEP IN MY BED AND I CAN NOT WAKE
UP.
- NO MATTER HOW LOUD I YELL, NO ONE CAN
HEAR ME. LIFE HAS A WAY OF SHOWING US
THINGS BEFORE THEY HAPPEN. WHAT DID YOU
LEARN?
- I LEARN THAT I SHOULDN'T GO TO SLEEP ON AN
EMPTY STOMACH, GET UP IN THE MIDDLE OF THE
NIGHT, AND SCREAM WHEN I OPEN THE REFRIGER-
ATOR AND SEE THAT SOMEONE DRANK THE LAST
LITTLE BIT OF MILK.
- YOU LEFT OUT ONE THING.
WHAT WAS THAT?
- THE BRIGHT LIGHT FROM WHEN
YOU OPEN THE REFRIGERATOR DOOR.
THAT WAS THE ETERNAL LIGHT.
SO, WHAT ARE YOU SAYING? I AM NOT DEAD.
- JUST THE OPPOSITE PARTNER.

LIKE THEY USE TO

PEOPLE DON'T HANG ON LIKE THEY USE TO. THEY
SEE THAT THE GOING IS GETTING ROUGH, AND
THEY JUST LET GO.

-I REMEMBER WHEN WE CAME TOGETHER, AND WE
SWORE THAT WE'D NEVER GIVE UP OR GIVE IN SO
EASILY, LIKE EVERYONE ELSE. THE FIRE WE HAD
BURN SO BRIGHTLY, OTHERS CAME FROM MILES
AROUND JUST TO TOUCH AND SEE.

- NOW, I AM SO GLAD THAT THIS RELATIONSHIP IS
OVER; I WAS GETTING RATHER TIRED OF HOLDING
MY BREATH EVERY TIME WE ARE TOGETHER. I KNOW
YOU MUST HAVE BEEN THE SAME WAY AS OF LATE. I
STARTED GETTING A HEADACHE WHENEVER WE
WERE TOGETHER.

- A PART OF ME WANTS TO STAY AND FIGURE THIS
WHOLE DAMN THING OUT, FEELING LIKE I AM GLUT-
TING FOR PUNISHMENT. I KEEP CERTAIN THINGS IN
MY HEART AND MIND THAT I JUST DON'T THROW
AWAY.

- ON THE FLIP SIDE OF THIS COIN, YOU LOSE. I
HAVE TO CONSIDER ME. IF I AM NOT GROWING, I
HAVE TO PACK YOUR BAGS OR MINES, BUT ONE OF
US HAS TO LEAVE.

YOU CAN'T

YOU CAN'T MAKE SOMEONE LOVE YOU. YOU CAN'T KEEP SOMEONE FROM LEAV-ING IF THEY WANT TO GO. LIFE IS TOO SHORT TO SPEND TIME WAITING ON SOMEONE ELSE, THAT'S NEVER HOME, AND WHEN THEY ARE, THEIR HEARTS ARE SOMEWHERE ELSE, ALONG WITH THEIR MINDS.

WE ALL NEED BODY, MIND, AND SPIRIT ALL IN ONE PLACE, EITHER WITH GOD OR ALL HERE WITH ME. I DON'T WANT TO HAVE TO GUESS WHERE YOU ARE IN THIS RELATIONSHIP.

LET ME KNOW WHEN YOU GET YOURSELF TOGETHER AND MAYBE I MIGHT BE ABLE TO PULL MYSELF TOGETHER; BODY, MIND, AND SPIRIT AND SHARE YOU WITH THE GOD I KNOW, THAT DOES NOT HAVE TIME FOR NON SENSE EITHER.

MOST MEN

MOST MEN KNOW
WHEN THEY'VE MESSED UP
A GOOD THING,
AND IT'S GONE.
WHEN THEY MAKE
A U-TURN YEARS LATER
THEY KNOW THEY WRONG.
THEY'RE HEAD MUST BE
IN THE CLOUDS, BECAUSE
SHE'S MOVED SO FAR AHEAD
OF YOU IN LIFE, SHE DOESN'T
NEED THE CIRCUS YOU BRING
TO TOWN, SHE JUST WANTS YOU
TO SPEND SOME TIME
WITH YOUR CHILD, AND KEEP
YOU CLOWN AZZ MOVING WITH
THE CIRCUS.
NOTHING LIKE A STRONG WOMAN
THAT REALIZES, THAT SHE DOESN'T
NEED A BROKE ASS MAN,
WITH NOTHING BUT SURPRISES.

OTHER CRACK-HEADS

YOU GIVE OTHER CRACK-HEADS A BAD
NAME. YOU DON'T BRUSH TEETH, YOU
DON'T BATHE, AND WHEN YOU DO, YOU
DON'T WASH YOUR ASS.

WHENEVER I TRY TO TALK TO YOU, YOU
KEPT TELLING ME THE SAME THINGS, THERE
ARE PEOPLE WATCHING YOU, AND FOLLOW-
ING ME ALL OVER TOWN.

THE OTHER DAY I SAW YOU DIRECTING
TRAFFIC WHILE STANDING ON THE DOUBLE
SOLID YELLOW LINES, WAVING A RED BLAN-
KET TOWARDS ONCOMING CARS LIKE A
MATADOR, BUT IN CHARISMATIC FORM. YOU
WERE WEARING A SAFARI HAT, A T-SHIRT
AND A PAIR OF BOXER SHORTS, WHICH
WERE BARELY HELD UP ABOVE YOUR KNEES.

I COULDN'T DO ANYTHING BUT CRY, KNOW-
ING MY BROTHER HAS LOST HIS WAY, AND I
DIDN'T KNOW HOW TO SAVE HIM. I THINK
RAYMOND'S WORLD HAS FINALLY COME
CRUMBLING DOWN. LET US ALL PRAY THAT
GOD COMPLETES THE WORK HE STARTED IN
US.

THE FIRST TIME WE MET

THE FIRST TIME WE MET
YOU HAD YOUR HANDS
ALL OVER ME.
I WAS INNOCENCE THEN,
SO IT MADE ME LAUGH.
I FELT A LITTLE NERVOUS,
BUT WHEN YOU KEPT
TELLING ME TO KEEP STILL,
AND TO KEEP QUIET.
I WAS THINKING,
YOU WERE HAVING
A BAD DAY.
NOW THAT I KNOW
THE SYSTEM,
AND BEEN THROUGH
THE SYSTEM.
I JUST LOOK INTO
YOUR EYES AND SAY
"WHAT SEEMS
TO BE THE PROBLEM
MS. OFFICER?"

BE THERE FOR YOU

I WANTED TO BE THERE
THE DAY YOU WERE BORN
BUT I COULDN'T MAKE IT
I WANTED TO BE THERE
WHEN YOU SPOKE YOUR
FIRST WORDS, I COULDN'T
MAKE IT.
I WANTED TO BE THERE TO
SEE YOU OFF ON THE FIRST DAY
OF SCHOOL, I COULDN'T MAKE.
I WANTED TO BE THERE FOR YOU
SIXTEENTH BIRTHDAY, I TRIED
BUT I JUST COULDN'T MAKE IT.
I KNOW YOU'RE ALL GROWN UP NOW
AND I HAVEN'T BEEN MUCH OF
A FATHER AND YOU SENT THIS
INVITATION TO YOUR CHILD'S
FIRST BIRTHDAY PARTY. BUT,
FOR THE CRIMES I'VE COMMITTED,
EXCEPT FOR YOUR CONCEPTION.
I JUST CAN'T MAKE IT.

LOVE IS A COLOR

LOVE IS A COLOR UNTIL IT START TO FADE.
-I THOUGHT FOR YEARS SHE LOVED ME, UNTIL
ONE DAY I DIDN'T FEEL THE LOVE ANYMORE.
-I THOUGHT SHE KEPT ME AROUND FOR MY
MONEY, UNTIL I FOUND OUT THAT SHE HAD
MORE THAN ME.
- I THOUGHT SHE MAY HAVE BEEN
CHEATING, BUT THAT WAS JUST CONSCIOUS
PLAYING TRICKS ON ME.
- I THOUGHT MAYBE SHE JUST KEEPS ME AROUND
BECAUSE I TAKE OUT THE TRASH, WASH THE
CLOTHES, AND PICK UP THE MORNING PAPER.
FOR WHATEVER REASON SHE HAD GOING ON IN
HER MIND, I WASN'T FEELING THE LOVE.
- IT TOOK ME A WHILE, AND I HAD TO WORK UP
THE NERVE BECAUSE I MIGHT NOT LIKE WHAT I
GOING TO HEAR. SO ASKED?
- BABE, CAN YOU TELL ME WHY I AM IN YOUR
LIFE?
BECAUSE YOU ARE THE ONLY MAN I KNOW THAT
WILL JUMP UP OUT OF BED, GO DOWN TWO
FLIGHTS OF STAIRS, RUN AROUND OUTSIDE IN
YOUR UNDERWEAR 3 O'CLOCK IN THE MORNING,
BECAUSE I SAID, I THINK I HEAR A NOISE. ALL
WHILE I AM ASLEEP, AND YOU KEEP ALL THE OTH-
ER MONSTERS AWAY. THAT'S WHY I LOVE YOU,
NOW GO BACK TO SLEEP.

USE TO GET BEATINGS

When we use to get beatings it use to hurt like hell, but back then there was no one you could kiss and tell. After a while it didn't matter what we did, we got the belt which left swell marks, and then we'd get up and run away, curse them and God, and found a place to hide.

I loved my dad out of respect, hate, and fear. Thanks to the lady next door who would sound off outside, "Luke leave those kids alone." Was always our saving grace. Lord knows we cried loud enough for the world to hear.

I wouldn't write this, if I didn't still feel him picking me up, and me wondering when is this whipping going to end? I felt it then and there's no one to stop me from saying it now. The crime didn't fit the punishment.

I can't wait until I get my turn to hold his ashes. I plan to return them to earth, from whilst they came. Then, maybe I can get some real sleep.

I Couldn't Get What I Wanted

I couldn't get what I wanted, so I got what I needed. But I still woke up wanting that thing I have been missing, and now I have to find a way to get you out of my head.

I realize in this slow economy that you're not the one for me. I understand your taste in organic foods and wearing fancy clothes, but right now my pockets are crying mercy, mercy me. I had to down grade my ride, so hoopdies are back in style.

Now, you don't even want me to pick you up because you are too good to be seen eating at McDonalds, wearing clothes from a near by mall, with a man that can't afford to make you happy.

I am not going to beat myself up, the decision has already been made, despite my situation, you are not the one for me. I am looking for that ride and die chick, that will hold my hand thru thick or thin, and would take in the air that I breathe, if that's what it takes. So when I was thinking about you, waiting on you, that was my first mistake. I can't get what I wanted and neither can you.

THIS IS WINTER

This is Winter, its nothing like what you would imagine.
Is it cold? Sometimes they come and take your blan-
ket away for no reason, while you are asleep. I tell my-
self, its only for a season.
Some days you have to managed walking around with
shoes on your feet that don't fit. It took everything
that I knew about Winter, and it made me forget.
Being locked up, you are constantly being told what to
do, where to stand, where to place your hands; and be
punished for following all the rules. This is Winter, my
conditions pain my body, mind, and spirit.
Its cold, very cold and I am trying to take a shower,
but I feel the chills of everyone staring at me
from my head to my toes.
I am a grown man but some perverted mind is taking
snapshots of me with their eyes. Even though it could
be raining, sleeting, or snowing, I don't get a taste of
the outside. I have written to everyone I know at
least five times, letting them know where I am, and
what days they can visit me. I would like to know
what's going on at home?

"It's hard not getting into my feelings if you can see what I am dealing with. Its cold my brother being locked up. no Winter is colder than this when they strip you of everything you know, and that's pretty damn brisk.

But, I received a document from the court and a visit from my lawyer the other day. That I will be getting out soon; and one of my babies' mommas told me she's looking forward to seeing me on an even day. Now that the weather outside is getting better I have an actual release date. I can see myself back on the streets hanging with my friends, playing ball on the court and making every attempt, not have to come in here again. This place is no place like home; that's why I look forward to Spring and getting away from this place I call Winter.

THE FAIRY TALE

Sorry, I missed the Fairy Tale beginning, and by the looks of it, it's not going to be a Fairy Tale ending. So, maybe I can start the story from the middle, and pray God for change. Once upon a time in the middle of the story, there are two people fussing and fighting, and throwing chairs at each other. Words are being exchanged, like, "I hate you, and You're worthless" and I don't love you anymore."

For some odd reason, those last few words were heard, and they sent a cold chill around the Angels in heaven. A small group of Angels conversed and said, "we must do something." By the time the fighting was done, she had packed up all her things, gathered the two young children, and was headed back home to her mother. I sat there in a daze, wondering where did this thing go wrong? I took my mind to an outer body experience to travel back in time. It was when we first met. My first opening line.

You sure look fine, from the front and the behind. I skipped a few years as things started to change. With the birth of each child, the increase of added stress of responsibility and the need for financial income. The distance became greater between us.

I saw less of her, and when I did, she was already asleep or up plastering me with more bills and lights out endless conversation about her day. Then before I can raise up out of my misery seat, I heard an Angel speak, "maybe I can help."

When you looked back, do remember how many times you prayed together, and ask God to keep you two together? Do you remember going to church on Sunday, when you had a problem and leaving it at the altar? God is a loving God. He only wants the best for you. But, if you don't include Him in your everyday life, He just figures, you don't need Him. What God does are answers prayers. So, if you want to change some things in your life to make it right. God is a game changer. But that's up to you if you want to live happily ever after.

MY CHILDREN

I love them, but I don't want to fight them. They've gotten to the point whereas they don't want to listen. I find myself talking to myself, and looking up and down the street for them, from the window. One day they will get it. I just want you to be safe out there.
Please don't waste any more of my time. It's okay to look my way, but don't stop to get my attention, don't even do anything to make me smile. I don't need any more headaches, hearts aches or head games; or days and nights trying to figure out what's on the other person mind.

Just leave me. I'd rather be left alone, than in a relationship with so much uncertainty. I know where I'm going, doesn't matter if I end up there alone. I've carried too much extra baggage, that didn't belong to me. I carried it a great distance, just to have to set it all down and walk away. It wasn't mines to carry.
Who wouldn't enjoy some light conversation every now and then, and being able to cuddle up beside a warm body? But, there has to be a lot more to it than that. I need the whole kit and caboodle, it can't be when I need the love in return, it turns ups and walks away.

MAD AT ME

Mad at me.
She's mad at me.
She's always mad at me.
It doesn't matter what
I say or what I do.

She's mad at me.
She's always mad at me.
I tried to talk to her calm and nice
it just doesn't matter.

She's mad at me.
She's always mad at me.
I don't go out and after work,
I come straight home.

She's mad at me.
She's always mad at me.
Why do I put up with her?
I don't know why but for right now,
I am mad at me.

I GOT IT

I've had dreams
And my dreams
have had me,
laughing, playing,
crying, running and
often times fighting.
Sometimes I'm making
love, other times love
is being made to me.
I have all kinds of dreams,
but the ones I am intrigued
the most by is the one
giving me a role in a story; often the
message is received the moment I
wake up or sometimes
the same dream is repeated like
a bad movie, until I wake up scream-
ing, "Lord, I got it!"

I AM A DREAMER

Hey pretty girl, you know you were always my
reality. It just that I was a dreamer that could
never stay awake long enough to enjoy your com-
pany when you were around. I miss all those spe-
cial moments we use to share kissing at the bus
stop and holding each other's hands like the
time was going to come when we'd never see
each other again.

I didn't know, had no idea that we'd go off in
our direction and that was the best way to end
things. Now, I spend a lot of time just looking
off in the distance reminiscing of days gone by
for good. No more rose petals leading up to your
bedroom, just for you. Or lit candles around the
edge of your bathtub, most certainly just for
you.

I hope when you wake up in the morning, in the
arms of your Lover, regrettably. I hope you
think of me and how we use to hold each other
like there was no tomorrow. And when the bus
finally arrives, the bus drivers open the door
asking, "Are you two going to get on? On just
keep carrying on?" I thought I would always be
there for you, to help make all your dreams come
true. Unfair was the wind that blew and changed
everything.

IT WAS ALWAYS YOU

It was always you. No matter how
many c o r n e r s I turned. It was al-
ways you in my heart and soul.

No matter how many bitter words
were exchanged, I felt the pain. It
was always you.

No matter how many times I fell in
another Lover's arms, I could never
swallow that moment, because they
weren't you. It was always you.

No matter how many times I couldn't
figure it out, and was filled with so
much doubt. You were always who all
my poems were about. They were al-
ways about you.

MINDLESS BEHAVIOR

The truth of the matter, I failed you by not giving you the best that's in me. I spent most of my time profitless negotiations and amusing myself in heartless love strings relationships. What do you want from me?

I am not a whole brand, name brand or an off brand. I am that brand that no one really wants, but everyone can afford, so you suffer the taste of where you are economically, which is often accompanied by comic released, once that internal gas hits you.

I got lost somewhere in my life between R Street and South Korea. I became a man but no one was there to mold me. I fell a few times and learned that I couldn't trust my eyesight or my heart.

Nothing appeared or lasted as I hoped, dreamed or imagined. So, if you ever wonder why I act or pretend the ways that I do. Simply, I got hurt, spent in circles, and then I vowed to myself that this will never happen again, so I run in opposition in all seriousness of commitment because I am afraid of being caught up or caught off guard, again.

LOVE IS A TWO WAY STREET

They say love is a two-way street but that's not with everyone you meet. Some folks live in singleness and they are single-minded. But sometimes we overwhelmed with there wit and charm, we are blinded. After a while, everything I was asking for was too much or burdensome.

So, I started second guessing everything I was doing, was wrong. Baby this, baby that, after a while all I could think about was not coming home right after work, or grabbing my coat and hat. My excuses became my way of life, I have something to do, I'll be right back, and the worst, don't wait up for me. For the first time, I could see my life going down a drain, and now I had no way to explain.

I tried almost everything before I found God. Figured, since I have failed at everything else, at least this is the way that it appeared. Never have I seen myself, overtaken by hurt and tears. If, we could just sit down and talk, and take time to listen to the other person. What a beautiful world this would be.

Did I mention, there are children involved and with them, the matter should easily be resolved. "Mommy, don't you still love daddy? and daddy don't you still love mommy?" I have never seen or heard quietness sit so still. To each their own, it's tough in this place we call home.

EVERYBODY HAS A STORY

Everybody has a story, but most of us don't want to tell our own. Too much for the world to know; it's easier to tell them a lie, and still wake up and feel good about ourselves.

It wasn't always so in the beginning, life inside a relationship was very good. Often, but unexpected things happen along the way, which caused me to reevaluate the way I look at the opposite sex, and how I hold their hand.

Irresponsible, I didn't act alone and didn't do this to me. It was my hope and intent to stay with the one I gave heart to the first time. But, it was given back to me fragmented.

Each time I tried to give it away, it became more difficult to put back together again. So now, I play it safe, all I do is play. I can't take anybody out here for serious I still pray, I ask God to help to find the missing pieces of my heart, so I can feel complete, love and live the way you intended me to. For those that have found love, hold onto them, for gems and rubies are a hard find in this world.

WINGLESS ANGEL

I DON'T EVEN THINK IT'S FUNNY

I don't even think its funny how other spirits won't rest and won't let us enjoy our time here on mother earth, without jumping up and down, knocking things down, vanishing and disappearing. You have convinced me, we are not alone here.

I don't like paying you any attention, my first instincts are to look and turn when I hear a thump or noise, but you've had your time here and if you are not resting, you took a wrong turn. Unfortunately for me, you're still unhappy and in a 'get back' mood.

Without me realizing it, I've allowed you to grow up with me, get inside my head and help me make some pretty bad decisions over the course of my life, and no I still down wasn't to talk to you aloud, because I don't want anyone to think I am going crazy, but fool, I know you are there.

I know how to get rid of you, you, you, and you, my goodness they are everywhere. I pray you away, I rebuke you in Jesus name. I don't sit and play chess games, waiting for you to make your next move.

I believe you have no place here and your only intention is to destroy the lives of others. Our children doing things they have no business, and it wasn't the way they were taught, marriages severed in half other vowing to be together for a lifetime, and people having disagreements with each other worlds apart, and they don't even know why.

I pray that you pray, not for just one or two, but for them all to go away. Pray God gives you strength and peace, and He restores the love that was lost in your home. I know everyone is not going to agree with me, but we all agree that we are not alone.

I DON'T BELIEVE

I don't believe in same-sex marriages, but I respect the unity that if two people want to be lawfully married. Then they should be, just not ordain in a church. I think we play too close to the line of what Gods intention are for our lives.

I am for Pro-Choice, with a Pro-Life voice for the one that can not speak for themselves, I believe they have as much of a right to sit at the Kings table as you do.

We are quick to convict a man with social behaviors but there aren't enough available or affordable programs. I can't wait until that time, where I can say, "My name is Ralph and I have a problem with."

Until that day, I will just stay in my closet as much as I can and pray God deliverers me.

Guns don't kill people, but guns in the wrong hands destroy lives.

I believe everyone has the right to bear arms, but it shouldn't be used unless you or someone in your home are in threat; and it has to be licensed, and go to a state-regulated FIRE-ARMS CLASS to learn the importance, every three years. I believe life is to be enjoyed, we just have to find the right way.

TUESDAY

We are not going to talk about Tuesday. I
looked at her while sitting on the edge of my
bed, I tried talking to her but she wouldn't
speak back to me.

I went out for a while but kept Tuesday on
my mind. I made my way to a coffee shop, en-
tangled in thoughts I tried desperately to
write them down. How can the pen speak to
paper, if it doesn't know what words it should
say? And why should the paper just lye
there, with hope, in expectation, while the
writer fails at his attempts and just walks
away?

I don't want it to end like this Tuesday,
there's just so much more inside of me. I
know, I know I have to satisfy you and meet
your every need. My effort to press and
please you will not go away. I need just a mo-
ment to think, add thought to my ink, so we
can move on to the next thing.

I WAS BORN BLACK

I was born Black
and I will die probably Black.
Regardless of
what I do or
don't do won't
change the
beginning or it's
ending color.
But what I can do
is change the way
people look at me,
and hopefully, they'll
see I'm no different
then they are,
inside or outside.
Hidden in today's society
are racism, prejudice, and
discrimination, and truly
we're robbing ourselves
and America's dream.
Too much of our heart's
foundation is banked in hatred.
I say, treat everyone with fairness,
and equality or as a family
member. Imagine what a wonderful
world this would be.

WE HAVE SURVIVED

Over the years we have survived through the in climate days of our lives; rainy days in Manhattan, unexpected snow on Long Island, the hottest July ever in the Bronx and a few close storms in Queens, that nearly almost tore us apart.

In the beginning, we were innocent and beautiful, now we're older and ugly, nobody wants me and they certainly aren't looking your way. We've had some great times while making incredible babies and a lot of foolish mistakes along the way but you know we managed to come together and pull each other up by the hand when it mattered the absolute most.

There have been days you've shouted me out of the house and with good probable cause, but the times we've embraced the moments of celebration made everything worth coming back together the while. As I have said in the very beginning, "I love you now, and forever after."

WITHOUT CLOSING THE DOOR

Every now and then, someone walks out our lives without closing the door. We often think we must have said or done something wrong, so we don't try to chase after them, we just let them go.

Now the pain has hit me because I understand, she needed someone to chase after her and never let her go. The love she sought after was someone that would be able to understand who she is, what she's gone thru, keep her from crying in the dark and make her smile when there's nothing to smile about.

It takes a while to really know a person, no matter how close you may think you are to them. When something tragic happens, all you can say is, I really didn't know them as well as I should have.

WRAP-UP SESSION

I just finished my morning wrap-up session with my son that's in High School. As I was driving I started and stopped myself before saying anything to him, as I am watching him play video games on his cell phone.

I want him to have a good day but I don't want to start it off in a bad way, so I turned my head forward to proceed with my driving.

So, before dropping him off and without any thoughtful consideration, I turned back to him and made him a monetary offer. That if you make the zeros disappear on School Max I will pay you this money on Friday.

He said, okay daddy, and without pausing he kept playing his video game. I ended the conversation by saying and pointing out that none of these children's parents pay their child for doing what they're supposed to be doing. I want to see you succeed in life. Have a good day son, "Okay daddy."

FLOWER AND ROSES

Good morning sunflowers and roses, I have to speak to you first, because you demand the greatest amount of attention and you bring the best out of others.

The world would be a much different place if there were no sunflowers or roses. These two together or apart changes a person heart, anytime they are given.

So thank you to my mother and grandmother for being the two special flowers in my life. You have given me nothing but joy and laughter, after all my childhood pain.

With all the whippings and spankings you've both earned my trust, and I promised to give my love and respect and to always put God first. I always say, good morning and thanks, for being in my life.

OUR HOUSE

Making mistakes is a human component but it doesn't have to be an exponent. And how we go about making the necessary corrections or changes are the challenges we face every day.

Many of us live with the mistakes we've made and don't need any reminders. Some of us have made the necessary corrections and moved on thankfully. I am forever apologetic to those I've hurt or fouled in the sport of the game.

I read my bible and made peace with God. My mom says, "Ralph, my son, mistakes happen, but you've got to try your best to avoid them. And try not to repeat them again."

Live, love and learn; make the best of every day and every opportunity. Mistakes happen, but more importantly what you do afterwards. I pray that you ask the offended and God for forgiveness. One Love.

SWISH

Swish bucket of tears all over the floor, as I looked away, there came more and more. This thing of watching them go off to school never seems to get old. I thought men didn't cry, she'll be my baby until I die.

I tried to hold onto her for as long as I possibly could, even I know I smothering her, I didn't want to let her. She told long ago, one day daddy, I am going to grow up and have to leave, and there's nothing you'd be able to do to stop me.

I laughed then, but I am not laughing now. The world outside my reach or arms has never been a safe place, so guess who's praying now. I know that she will be better than okay. The hardest part for me is looking forward and walking away.

In times past I would sit in the parking lot or around the corner just in case she's forgotten something or needs another hug. I told her I wasn't going to miss her after I was gone. I was right again, I miss her already, and I haven't even left the parking lot at Bowie State University.

My best to her and all she hopes to accomplish. And without saying, one of my angels will stay behind and keep watch over daddy's little girl. She doesn't know it, but in help raising her, I became a better me.

WHAT ARE BROTHERS FOR?

What are brothers for? My mother and father always said, watch your brother, and make sure he doesn't hurt himself and don't let them get into any trouble. Or I will hold you personally responsible.

After I grew up, I left home and went straight into the United States Marine Corps. Every day was pretty much the same. They yelled and screamed that we're brothers and all a team. And nowhere else in the world will you find, "No man left behind."

To the depths of hell and/or up to the steps of heaven, I will come and get you, my brother. Without another word from those that have always been in my ears. With tears I am praying for my brother and that my prayers save him.

What I had to learn without confusion, that if you want to successfully rescue someone or anyone, you have to go in and come away with Jesus as your covering.

TWO MEN

Two men sitting in jail, one was exclaiming how he
got caught. Both aware of the other's convic-
tions. While the other inmate that had been
housed longer listened. Afterward, after many
hours later, he spoke.

I hope that before you leave this imprisonment
or in this life, that you learn to listen. We're
both here because we ignored all the people along
the way and including God, We made the choice
to rob, steal, or kill; victimizing the lives of peo-
ple that love us and of perfect unaware
strangers.

For those that are on the outside of these walls
of redemption and salvation, your day will come
and you will be judged. Because you didn't get
caught, you still will be held accountable for your
sins.

Though, I might be locked up now, I'm paying for
my faults. I know when I leave here, I'll see
heaven afterward. I pray that you ask God for
forgiveness before you end up in a far worse
place than where I am right now.

DAD

Though those that are very close to me would never know it, I loved my father. I got tired of trying to win his approval and acceptance. It came a little too late to my ears to hear him say, "I'm proud of you son." By then my heart didn't need the fuel for the fire.

The one thing I did do as I grew up from a child to a man, was love and respect him regardless of our differences, and we had our differences.

While the world still misses this man years after his death, and I respect them for that. But no matter how hard I try, I can't get this man out of my house.

So each day we walk and talk, and I'm still being respectful. He still smokes Kool cigarettes and drinks coffee. And before I can formulate into words, he's already put down on paper. Him being one the worlds least recognized writers.

My footsteps are his footprints carrying me each step of the way. As I look down at the footprints in the sand they appear even deeper as I carry my son. My dad always being the tough guy has never put me down, his Soldier's Creed.

LEARNING ABOUT
THE KINGDOM

IT TOOK ME A LONG WHILE TO LEARN WHAT THE KINGDOM OF GOD IS ALL ABOUT. I STILL DON'T HAVE ALL THE ANSWERS, AND I HAVE A LONG WAYS TO GO.

SO I SAY, "IN ALL YOUR GETTING, GET UNDERSTANDING," AND "LEAN NOT TO YOUR OWN UNDERSTANDING," AND SEEK HIM EARLY.

I AM MORE THAN A CONQUEROR THROUGH CHRIST JESUS WHO STRENGTHENS ME, "I KNOW WHERE MY HELP COMES FROM."

ON THIS DAY, I PRAY THAT YOU GET TO KNOW THE LORD IN A BETTER WAY. BE ENCOURAGED AND KNOW THAT HE LOVES YOU.

THE BIG PICTURE

I am not too afraid to admit, that there were many times
I missed God's big picture. I was always too busy doing
something else or looking in the other direction. Only
when I stepped back, the big picture was perfectly clear.
I looked up and said, "God what do you want from me?"
Life is about learning how to love more than just yourself.
Learning to care for those inside and outside your village.

I know it's hard when it is so much easier being busy doing
what you want to do or simply looking the other way. Be-
cause this happenstance has occurred many times. I had
to search the depths of my soul. Lord, I found myself
standing in murky water.

I wanted to blame the world first for all my shortcomings,
and tell you why the child in me is still angry, and tell you
the endless stories about how we went without while
growing up.

Nobody has heard me I sing hymns to my spirit about how
I deserve so much more. I really didn't need God to tell
me, that I am shallow. Again Dear Lord, as I give thanks
to you for waking me up, I will try to do better.

As I looked down at my tears falling, the murky water be-
came clearer. I felt His grace once again. He always
speaks to me and touches me like a friend. I pray that He
doesn't have to keep waking me up out of my sleep, but I
don't mind having the conversations. The big picture was
made clear, I will do better.

SHELTER

I need shelter, and people have their place and ne-
cessities, but God will bring you out and keep you
out, but you have to hold on and keep your faith. I
can give you and others can you give what you want,
but Jesus will give you what you need. I will pray for
you, I have prayed for you but you have to surren-
der to His will.

That means you have to listen to His voice and be
obedient. Because if you don't listen to Jesus and
you're not being obedient, how can you expect a
change? You're always going to have a story, and
it's going to make some people cry, and a few will
pray on your behalf and ask God why?

But, I've been around God long enough to know, that
if you ever find yourself in a particular place or way
down low, you have to find ways to increase your
faith and you never get out of God's face. Don't let
the devil use you.

People will try to help you, but these amenities will
only last for a little while, but when you have Jesus,
His love will sustain you and I for a lifetime. I can't
say it enough or loud enough, that p r a y e r chang-
es everything.

FOSTERING

I HAVE BEEN FOSTERING HOPES THAT ONE DAY THINGS WILL GET BETTER BETWEEN YOU AND ME. SOMETIMES WHEN I PRAY, I GET DOWN ON BOTH KNEES, AND CLASP MY HANDS TOGETHER AND LOOK UP TOWARDS HEAVEN. I DON'T QUESTION GOD, BUT I THINK WITHIN MYSELF, WHY?

I ALWAYS WANTED THIS THING TO WORK OUT BETWEEN US, EVEN AFTER WE REALIZE THAT WE ARE THE BLAME. I THOUGHT IF SOMETHING WAS BROKEN MOST OF THE TIME IT CAN BE FIXED AGAIN.

I DONT KNOW HOW TO BEND ANY FURTHER WITHOUT TENDERING EVENTUALLY ALONG THE WAY. WHAT HAPPENED TO THE LOW OR NO EXPECTATIONS? I GUESS IT WENT OUT THE DOOR AND WINDOW WITH THE REST OF MY STUFF.

I AM ON CLOUD # 9

If you don't know, it's a really good feeling and a really nice place to be once you arrive. I may not be where I want to be in life, and the person beside me still doesn't quite understand me.

My life steps look crazy at any distance, because I'm avoiding all my haters, the nay-sayer and those setting mind traps out there, by asking me, what's my name? What's my number?

Then a list of bullshit other questions. I know you're reading me, because I'm reading you. I see and feel some of my best friends are getting off Facebook and other social media, for a list of other reason I have yet to mention. I'm in a happy place, like you. I don't want people trying to reel me in like a fish, by using fresh bait.

Yes, I'm a little hungry in certain areas in my life but over and over, my mom and dad didn't raise no dummies. The Internet is not your friend, so be very careful who befriends you out there. I pray that you pray, "God give me the vision to see what's out there." And, if you don't know, ask somebody or shut the computer off.

BIRTH - DEATH

They have this beautiful thing that God freely gives us between birth and death, it's called life. It matters because its an afforded opportunity for everyone to make something of themselves, and it should not be squandered.

We come into this world not knowing anything but with a spirit to learn. Many of us have the privilege of being born into a family with a loving mother, father, grandparents, or guardians but you and I both know that's not everyone's situation.

But still, the opportunity of a breath of air does exist to profit and move forward in all of us. You're here now, regardless of what you have or don't have. We all have to find our own destiny, become resolved from whatever issues, mishaps or happenstances that may surround or distorted our perspective.

Seek to stay focus on the long road ahead, know what your goals are in life and try to avoid the pit holes by making pit stops along the way. I am talking about the influences that may factually take you out of the game. Things that make you miss your mark.

Some of these things seem okay in the very beginning, and then the gravity of all its related negativity pulls you in. I am talking about lying to your parents, swearing amongst your friends, drinking when you think no one is looking, having unprotected sex, and associating yourself with drugs in any capacity. These are common distractions but the influences of their consequences can be sickly, traumatic, incarceration, and deathly.

At what point did we stop listening to our parents, the pastor, our teachers, or anyone in our village? We know that we need be more responsible, but we shouldn't keep allowing our fate to be decided by our wrongdoings. And from never reaching our destiny because of the foolish choices or poor decisions we made along the way.

So in retrospect, I want to be the best parent for any child that I can be. Make something of yourselves, try to avoid the pit holes by taking the pit stops of anything or anyone trying to get you to do things that you know are not lawfully right, that I've been taught better or you've learned in church.

I don't want to have to come to visit you sick in the hospital, laying in the streets, or in the morgue. Child of God, I was once a child, know this, the road ahead is far better than the influences of their consequences and being careful is not enough.

Because even the best of us eventually get caught or caught up, without realizing until years later that we've missed our opportunity to make something of ourselves. Between those two points of birth - death.

I CAME INTO THIS WORLD

I came into this world.
I knew my mom,
but I never knew
my dad.
I love my mom,
she did an awesome
job raising me.
I just wanted to know
what would it be like,
if I had a dad?
He was never there
for me all my life.
A bastard child.
Silent tears,
this was never fair,
especially when you knew
I existed in this world.
For all the absentee dads,
I pray to your heavenly father to forsake
you also, especially when you
need him.

READING THOUGHTS

When you look at me I can read your thoughts.
You're thinking, something is seriously wrong with
him. Look at the way he walks.

Listen to the way he talks and all their clothes
are like nothing I'd wake up any day of the week
and put on. I don't believe they are from around
here. Why don't they go home?

Weird as it may seem, I am praying they can read
my thoughts but I'd be wrong for my thoughts,
especially spoken aloud.

Everyone in God's kingdom has a right to roam
until they choose a home. Even Jesus packed up
His belongings and left Galilee.

Where am I right now? Praying for your salvation
again. Forgive them, Father, for they know not
again what they do when they ridicule those that
are different from themselves. We are all your
children, aren't we?

D.C. Native Son
13 Self Published
Books
Available on Amazon
Ralph Watkins / Poet

WINGLESS ANGEL

www.ingramcontent.com/pod-product-compliance
Lightning Source LLC
LaVergne TN
LVHW041232080426
835508LV00011B/1171